The Forgotten Factor

Placing Community at the Heart of Mission

Mark Berry

Church Mission Society Community Mission Mobiliser
and Pioneer Leader of the Safespace Community, Telford

Philip Mounstephen

Executive Leader, Church Mission Society

GROVE BOOKS LIMITED
RIDLEY HALL RD CAMBRIDGE CB3 9HU

Contents

Acknowledgments
Safespace community members and friends past and present. Anyone and everyone who attended, in whatever capacity, Pathfinder Ventures at Riddlesworth Hall, Abbots Bromley, Perrott Hill or Sidmouth 1998–2006.

First Impression February 2017
ISSN 2399–6536
ISBN 978 1 78827 002 1

Getting the Issue on the Agenda

For both of us, as people committed to mission, community—as a concept and a commitment—is not an optional extra or an adjunct. For us both it is essential, not least because we are both members of the Church Mission Society community, a community whose members commit themselves to live a life of mission. If the mission of God is the calling of the church of God then community and mission cannot be separated. And yet so often they have been. The (mainly western) image of the evangelist as the lone hero has not helped. To neglect community is to weaken our mission. In this opening chapter we will each start from our own perspective and explain just why it is that community matters to us in mission.

PM: In summer 1998, I spent ten days as a leader on a Christian summer camp for 11–14 year olds—and a wonderful time I had too. I went for the next couple of years, and enjoyed it more and more. And then, in 2000, the overall leaders asked me to take over from them. These were good people who had done an outstanding job, and while I knew I had to accept, I was worried. It is a daunting thing to take overall responsibility for a residential holiday for some 70 young people and 40 adults. There is so much that can go wrong.

But take it over I did, and that first summer we had a great time. When it was all over, I asked myself why it was so good. Yes, we had a fantastic site, a beautiful old house in the middle of the countryside, we had some wonderful young people, we had an excellent programme of activities, and we had a great leadership team. But somehow the whole thing seemed like more than the sum of its parts. And then it struck me. What we had done, quite unintentionally, was to build a community. That was what we became over those few days: a community. That was why at the end it was so hard to leave, and why there were so many tears—we were breaking what had become quite deep bonds of community.

What we had done, quite unintentionally, was to build a community

So in the years that followed we set about not being accidental but being quite deliberate about building community. We did not just want it to happen; we wanted to *make* it happen—or rather we wanted God to make it happen, in our midst. And of course we did not want to be any old community: we wanted to be a *Christian* community. We wanted to build something truly different, something truly Christian, a place where God was at work amongst us. That is what we wanted to build. That is what we wanted to *be*.

I would not say we always succeeded but I do believe that, with God's help, we did do something really quite significant that made a real impact on the lives of many young people, and on many leaders. And it made a real impact on me. I think God used that experience to open my eyes to something we all too often lose sight of in our contemporary discipleship, and that is the precious concept of community, a subject which all too often we have treated as an optional extra in Christian living, but which is, I believe, absolutely fundamental to our being Christians.

Year after year, amidst all those tears at the end of camp, young people would come up to me and ask, 'Philip, why can't church be more like this?' And at first I would make excuses and fob them off. But I repented of that, and said, 'That's a very good question. It should be, and it can be.' And I believe it should be and can be and I believe passionately that if church is failing as community, it is not only failing its members, it is failing those who do not belong to it, it is failing in mission and thus it is failing the Lord himself.

Community for me will never be an optional extra

So community for me will never be an optional extra. Rather, as we will show in these pages, it is fundamental both to Christian identity and to Christian mission.

MB: In 2001 I took up a position as a deanery youth minister in Buckinghamshire. Part of the role was to bring the young people in the churches across the deanery together. It became very clear early on that this was going to be quite a challenge. The young people came from right across a deanery that did not fit together; it sat between three major towns with three very different cultures: Aylesbury, Buckingham and Milton Keynes. The young people had completely different stories: some lived in affluent villages, some were public school educated; others lived on the fringes of the urban, multicultural conurbations and attended the local state schools.

It was obvious that to treat this group of young people as one culture was going to be impossible. To lead them through a discipleship course or programme was going to alienate some, however we led it. Not only were their lifestyles radically different from each other's, so were they to my own. How then was this group going to function? The answer was it could not, at least not as a group. We could not find a lowest common denominator that would not frustrate one section or another; we had to find a way which took us all to a new place.

As we began together to work this out, we started to listen to each other and share ideas. We discovered that we did not need anyone to mediate or teach; we could all learn from everyone else, including me, as we sought to dwell in the Bible and see ourselves as participants and players in the ongoing story. The model of learning we were all used to was that of the classroom / lecture hall, where an expert imparts knowledge and then tests the learners. What we found was that there were no experts and we were all experts—we all had wisdom based on our varied experiences and we all had perspectives which shone light on how we sought to live as disciples. Discipleship became, then, not a school room but a shared practice. This is not to say chaos reigned, rather we explored a number of practices of theological reflection and, using these models, challenged each other to dig deeper and learn. We discovered community learning…

Through this experience we discovered community; we became invested in each other. We began to learn to see each other in a new way and in doing so we began to see God in a new way. As we argued and had to find forgiveness for each other we had a new glimpse of God's grace; as we had to learn to trust each other with our deepest vulnerabilities and move both deeper into them and beyond them, we encountered the self-surrender at the heart of the Trinity. As we saw the creativity in each other and shared the gifts each of us had, we caught something of the joy of real community. That is not to say being community is easy; on the contrary, it is hard work. It requires a certain amount of self-sacrifice and deep patience at times. But I discovered something that is now at the root of my faith—that we were not only better together, but each of us found out more about who we really were in relationship. Community is not best practice; it is a not a solution or a strategy; it is who we were made to be—in the image of a God who is community. As Archbishop Tutu once said, 'I am only truly me, because we are we.'

Those of us born and raised in western, minority culture are the children of individualism. Our culture has taught us that if we focus on the individual, on ourselves, then the rest will fall into place. The word 'personal' has become central in our missiology and indeed our eschatology: personal relationship with God, personal salvation. As we dwell in the whole of Scripture we find a bigger, more global picture: a picture of *shalom*, meaning wholeness or com-pleteness, and the notion of *shelemut*, of perfection. This cosmic reconciling and recreating mission of God begins in Genesis and flows through the whole of the Bible. Faithful community, then, as we will go on to explore, can be said to be both the *method* of God's mission (see, for instance Deut 28.9–10; John 13.34) and the *purpose* of it (Rom 8.14–17) as God restores his *shalom* (Col 1.19–20).

2

The Biblical Foundations of Mission Community

Ultimately community is important because it reflects both the nature and the activity of God. And of course the two are related. God builds community because he is community, in his essence.

The foundational Christian understanding of God is that he is holy Trinity: three in one. He is himself, in the words of John Zizioulas, 'being as communion.'[1] Because God is three in one and one in three, because he is one God, Father, Son and Holy Spirit, there is intimate community, a community of love at the heart of God. It is what he is. And of course what he is, his people are to be, that his character might be formed in them. In Mike Lowe's words,

God is, throughout Scripture, in the business of creating community

'Creating community is at the heart of the Christian theological tradition in the doctrine of the Trinity. Individualism, separateness and fragmentation give way to individuality, mutuality and belonging.'[2]

And because God the Holy Trinity is himself community, he is, throughout the narrative of Scripture, in the business of creating community.

Genesis studiedly and deliberately relates the creation of man as male and female to the nature of God himself, with the distinct suggestion that the complementarity of the sexes is necessary in order fully to reflect the *imago dei* (Gen 1.27). Being in community is essential if the divine likeness is to be fully expressed. God only pronounces one thing not good before the fall. It is not good for the man to be alone: he needs community. And that community expands in response to the divine injunction to 'be fruitful and increase in number' (Gen 1.28).

The story of Israel in the OT is a community story. It is a family history flowing from the marriage of Adam and Eve, through the story of the patriarchs, into the exodus, through the time of the judges, the kings, the exile and the return. All that is a family, a community, story.

It is now widely accepted that the old idea that the New Testament is much more individualistically focused than the Old—a conviction probably fuelled by Reformation concerns about individual justification by faith—has been largely discredited. Indeed the NT is firmly communal in its outlook.

From the start Jesus is in the business of building community as he gathers a ragtag group of people, often intentionally remodelling the community of Israel around him, as in the choosing of 12 disciples. Community is central to Jesus' preaching of the kingdom: 'Jesus presents us with a dream (embodied in the group image 'kingdom of God') that is irreducibly communal, familial and social…It is a dream of a community vibrant with life, pulsating with forgiveness, loud with celebration, fruitful in mission…a substantial city whose streets bustle with life, whose buildings echo with praise, a city aglow with the glory of community.'[3]

Jesus' instinct is always to include and he castigates the Pharisees for excluding people from the community. And that challenging instinct to include is what ultimately leads him to the cross. But of course it is, ironically, through the cross that the community of grace becomes truly inclusive, including ultimately not only Jews, but gentiles too.

And as in the life of Jesus so in the life of the early Christian communities founded in his name. Paul's extended 'body' illustration in 1 Corinthians 12 is designed to demonstrate how ministry happens in the local church, and it suggests that it is in the context of diverse community that ministry is most effectively exercised. But there is an added theological twist. The work of God thrives and flourishes in the context of community because, Paul says, God is especially present in the context of community. This is not any body: this is the body *of Christ* that he is talking about, a community in which his character is being formed. And the abiding image at the end of Scripture is not of God in glorious lofty isolation, but surrounded by the saints at worship in heaven: a community drawn from every nation, tribe, people and language (Revelation 7).

The community God creates and indwells does not exist for its own sake. Starting with Adam and Eve, the calling of both old and new covenant people is to be a blessing to the whole world (and by extension to all creation). It is an inclusive vocation—to bless *all*. In Isaiah 42, in the context of proclaiming himself the God who has created all the earth (v 5), the Lord outlines the missional vocation of Israel: 'I have given you as a covenant to the people, a light to the nations, to open the eyes that are blind, to bring out the prisoners from the dungeon, from the prison those who sit in darkness' (Isa 42.6–7).

Community exists to be a blessing to the whole world

The covenant with Abraham and the promise to give him the land is tied up with the vocation to be a blessing to the whole world (Gen 12.3). And the New Testament parallel is that the gift of the Spirit (as opposed to the land) in Acts 1 is tied up with the calling to be Jesus' witnesses to the ends of the earth. The calling of both old and new covenant people is to be a blessing to the whole world.

We can see this critical connection between community and mission in particularly sharp focus in Acts 2.42–47. There is a direct connection between this snapshot of the fledgling Christian community we see at the end of Acts 2 and the gift of the Holy Spirit at Pentecost we hear described in the opening verses of that chapter. Indeed, in the light of the gift of the Spirit this description of the fledgling church is much more than a snapshot: it is a blueprint; this is what Christian community formed and shaped by the Holy Spirit is *supposed* to look like.

In the last half century or so much discussion about the ministry of the Holy Spirit, at least in the western church, has focused on the gifts the Spirit gives us *individually*. And there have been good reasons why there has been that focus. But the first manifestation of the ministry of the Spirit coming out of the events of Pentecost is that a *community* is formed.

The Holy Spirit creates a community in which, unsurprisingly, the fruit of the Spirit are very much in evidence. This is a place of love, joy, peace, patience, kindness, goodness, faithfulness, gentleness and self-control (Gal 5.22, 23). The Holy Spirit creates a community of devotion both to God and to each other; a place in which belonging mattered much more than having: a true community of the Spirit.

This community can thus be seen as a fulfilment of the prophecy and promise of Jesus in John 14. Jesus promises his disciples the gift of the Spirit. And when the Spirit comes 'you will know that I am in the Father, and you in me, and I in you' (v 20). This is an image of the intimate community which the Spirit creates. And that intimacy is emphasized in v 23, 'Those who love me will keep my word, and my Father will love them, and we will come to them, and make our home with them.' The community which the Spirit creates is a place of intimacy in which we are not only at home with one another but at home, with all that that implies, with the Lord himself.

The community the Spirit creates is a place of mission

And to go back to the community we see described in Acts, the community the Spirit creates is not only a place of intimacy, it is also a place of mission—or rather *because* it was a place of intimacy it was also a place of mission. These first Christians did not set about intentionally to engage in mission: it just happened, effectively as a by-product of the intimacy they experienced: 'and day by day the Lord added to their number those who were being saved' (Acts 2.47). That should not surprise us. There is something powerfully attractive and missional about genuine Christian community.

So community matters. Community is not an optional extra, but is essential to everything it means to be a Christian, because we are not called to be Christians alone but together, and together we are invited into the community of love at the very heart of God—that through the quality of our community others too might find themselves at home in the love of the Lord. This is what the Holy Spirit does: he creates community, he fills that community and he draws other people into that community. That in a nutshell *is* the ministry of the Holy Spirit: the creation of missional community, as a reflection and an extension of the community of love at the heart of God.

A ministry in the power of the Spirit ought to be deeply concerned with the creation of such community. Our experience is that when we are intentional about building community we do indeed see growth. There is a certain evangelical reluctance, perhaps, to organize events that do not have obvious purpose. Our experience, however, is that time spent playing, dancing and eating together (the kind of things for which Jesus was castigated) is never wasted. Such activities are purposeful in that they build community, and they build community that grows.

To offer one small illustration: when Philip led an open youth club in the town he once lived in they always started with half an hour or so just relaxing, chatting, and playing games together. His co-leader, wanting to get the more formal aspect of the evening underway (which would certainly involve some teaching and learning) would often say to him, 'Philip, don't you think we should start?' And he would always reply, 'We already have.' And they had, because what they did in that half hour established friendships, strengthened relationships—and built community.

3 The Two Structures of God's Redemptive Mission

David Bosch wrote in 1992 that, 'During the last half century…the classical doctrine of the *missio Dei* as God the Father sending the Son, and God the Father and the Son sending the Spirit was expanded to include yet another "movement": the Father, Son and the Holy Spirit sending the church into the world. As far as missionary thinking was concerned, this linking with the doctrine of the Trinity constituted an important innovation…Mission is thereby seen as a movement from God to the world; the church is viewed as an instrument for that mission. There is church because there is mission, not *vice versa*. To participate in mission is to participate in the movement of God's love toward people, since God is a fountain of sending love.'[4]

The church, according to Bosch, is drawn into this mission movement of the Trinity. The church itself is sent; the community is the mission of God and it participates in the mission of God, through the Son, with the Spirit. Therefore not only is the church drawn into God's mission, but as co-adopted heirs it shares the inheritance and therefore ownership of this mission. God's mission is now the church's mission. So the church is fulfilling its very nature as it participates in God's mission movement.

The community is the mission of God

But the Christian community has, since its earliest days, existed in two forms, both of which are essential for mission. These two forms are what Ralph Winter, in an address given to the All-Asia Mission Consultation in Seoul, Korea, in August 1973, called 'modality' and 'sodality.'

The first structure in the New Testament scene is thus what is often called the New Testament church. It was essentially built along Jewish synagogue lines, embracing the community of the faithful in any given place.

There is a second, quite different structure in the New Testament context. While we know very little about the structure of the evangelistic outreach within which pre-Pauline Jewish proselytizers worked, we do know, as already mentioned, that they operated all over the Roman Empire.

Thus, on the one hand, the structure we call the *New Testament church* is a prototype of all subsequent Christian fellowships where old and young,

Because both modes are essentially missional in focus, Winter calls them, 'the two structures of God's redemptive mission.' He uses the term modality to refer to the local church: multi-generational and geographically limited with a long-term commitment to its community. The second structure, the sodality, focuses on a movement with a specific focus with a secondary commitment to move beyond the local, such as his 'missionary-band.'

Both these structures are built on an understanding that the nature of church, both modal and sodal, is community. The former, a located and embedded community, deeply committed to the place and the people it finds itself amidst; the latter, a semi-autonomous, pioneering community willing to go wherever it is called. Yet both modes have a clear missional vocation.

In both Deuteronomy and in the early Jerusalem church we can see a strong image of the modal community, called to be visible as a community centred on God in a specific location. This calling is no easy one; it requires the community to be transparent and exposed. In John 13.34, 35 the focus is on reflecting Christ's love: 'Love one another. As I have loved you, so you must love one another. By this everyone will know that you are my disciples, if you love one another.' Love is not a superficial emotion or act, especially when set against the sacrificial and sacramental love of Christ. To be community means seeking this level of radical mutuality, learning through disagreement, even conflict, wrestling with deep forgiveness and healing. Doing this in the exposure of the local is the great challenge and the missional call of the modal community.

Walter Brueggemann in his 1982 book, *Living Toward a Vision: Biblical Reflections on Shalom*, writes that this call is heard most audibly around the table.[6] The communion draws our eye to God incarnate and sacramental, to a sent God and a sacrificial God, a God who creates in community, who redeems in community and who sustains in community. It is no surprise then that we find ourselves deepest in God when we are in community, when we find ourselves loving others, forgiving others, seeing God in others, giving ourselves in surrender to others and, significantly, breaking bread with others.

It would be a mistake, therefore, to undervalue the missional potential of the modal community: that potential is clearly illustrated in Acts 2.42–47, as we saw in chapter two. Bevans and Schroeder reference Orthodox theologians Stamoolis and Ion Bria when they say, 'Liturgy (the Eucharist) is always the entrance into the presence of the triune God and always ends with the community being sent forth in God's name to transform the world in God's image. Mission is conceived, in other words, as "the liturgy after the liturgy," the natural consequence of entering into the divine presence in worship.'[7]

Samuel Torvend writes in his book, *Daily Bread, Holy Meal*, of the importance of 'Breathing in and breathing out.'[8] He uses two laws of physics to illustrate this, the centripetal—or inward—force and centrifugal—or outward—force. Both are essential to a modal community:

> Christian worship often looks deeply centripetal: that is, people seek a 'peaceful' centre; they are drawn inward, away from a world that may appear threatening. It is no surprise that the assembly, which is a body, must breathe in air, drink water, and ingest food in order to survive. The centripetal movement of the liturgy draws people into the centre of Christian worship and its supper. Yet one of the core insights of Luther is the insistence that in the Lord's Supper Jesus Christ is given for the life of the world. Luther says, 'As love and support are given you, you in turn must render love and support to Christ in his needy ones.' Luther clearly announces the centrifugal movement of the liturgy and the Christian assembly. Along with breathing in, the body must also breathe out in order to survive. Set next to the centripetal movement of gathering inward is the centrifugal movement of sending outward into a beautiful yet threatening world.'

The church in Antioch we see in Acts 11 and 13 is a classic example of a modal community, breathing in and breathing out; giving expression to both the centripetal and centrifugal dynamics. Antioch was the third city of the Roman Empire, after Rome and Alexandria, the capital of the province of Syria a few miles up the river Orontes from its port Seleucia. In the city there were people from all kinds of cultural and ethnic backgrounds, from as far away as Africa, India and China. The Christians who came to the city, who themselves came from cosmopolitan places such as Cyprus and Cyrene, shared the good news of Jesus not just with their fellow Jews but with Greeks as well, with non-Jews. These are people who in the terms of orthodox Judaism were beyond the pale, but who astonishingly, we are told, respond to the good news of Jesus in considerable numbers, and so find themselves no longer on the outside looking in, but incorporated within the church, this amazing community, which is taking shape in Antioch. They are drawn in, breathed in, into community.

The church in Antioch is a classic example of a modal community

This church was a reflection of the place and people it came from; as diverse a place as Antioch itself, a community of Jews and gentiles, with wide cultural roots. 'Simeon called Niger' who we hear about in 13.1 was black: that is what 'niger' means. This was a genuinely ethnically and culturally diverse church that grew up in the city. It was quite unlike the very monocultural church in Jerusalem.

Indeed this church was a challenge to the church in Jerusalem, so its leaders sent Barnabas to Antioch to verify its authenticity. Barnabas knew the grace of God when he saw it so he rejoiced in what he found. He stayed in Antioch and played his part in building up the church, with the result that even more people were added to this rich modal community.

But then a significant change takes place: a sodal community is born out of this modal church as Paul, Barnabas and John are released for the work of mission.

Up to now the good news has come to be spread through either circumstances such as persecution, or through the direct intervention of the Lord, for instance by sending Philip to meet the Ethiopian eunuch in Acts 8. But now the church takes direct action in launching this mission movement and commissioning Paul and Barnabas for it.

It is the Holy Spirit who takes the initiative in this as he tells the church to set these two men aside for mission. This church was clearly waiting expectantly on the Lord for him to act: they fast and pray both before and after the Spirit speaks to them. But nonetheless the church takes a much more active role in initiating this work of mission than has ever happened before. It is the first time the church has really deliberately 'breathed out' in mission.

Paul and Barnabas became a sodal expression of church

Paul and Barnabas were still part of the church when they left Antioch and set out on mission. They were no longer part of that local, gathered, modal community, but they had not left the church. They became a sodal expression of church and certainly remained a part of, and a legitimate expression of, the one holy catholic and apostolic church. Indeed they were demonstrating the apostolic, sent, nature of the church.

So we have here two expressions of the church of God: the gathered modal church in mission in Antioch and the scattered or sent church in mission expressed in the sodal community of Paul, Barnabas and John Mark. And these two expressions of church, the modal and the sodal, are both entirely legitimate as expressions of church, and both have a distinct role to play in enabling the church to fulfil its mission. It is essential, therefore, that we have a mission ecclesiology that embraces both. Both of them are legitimate, complementary and necessary expressions of church.

And not just in Acts, but throughout Christian history we can see how essential the church in sodal form has been: scattered in movements of mission. We see this in mission movements as varied as Celtic monks in the so-called dark ages who shared the gospel across much of Europe; or Catholic movements such as the Jesuits who played such a key role in evangelism in parts of the world centuries before any Protestant missionaries got there, or the Moravians or the Methodists. All through history the Lord has raised up such mission movements from within his church and used them to spread the good news of his kingdom. What we see in Antioch sets the pattern for what is to follow not just in Acts but throughout Christian history. Indeed there has never been a significant advance in mission without the involvement of such groups. The failure of the Protestant churches after the Reformation to grasp the great significance of such mission movements meant that there was a gap of nearly 300 years before they launched out in global mission. Meanwhile, of course, Catholic sodalities such as the Jesuits had been active in mission all through the seventeenth and eighteenth centuries.

The Church Mission Society is of course one such sodal mission movement. Ralph Winter describes the early Church Missionary Society, under the influence of Henry Venn, in these terms: 'Toward the latter half of the nineteenth century, there seemed increasingly to be two separate structural traditions. On the one hand, there were men like Henry Venn and Rufus Anderson, who were the strategic thinkers at the helm of older societies—the Church Missionary Society (CMS) in England and American Board of Commissioners for Foreign Missions (ABCFM), respectively. These men championed the semi-autonomous mission sodality, and they voiced an attitude, which was not at first contradicted by any significant part of the leaders of the ecclesiastical structures. On the other hand, there was the centralizing perspective of denominational leaders.'

The creative and dynamic interplay between the modal and sodal is vital for mission

This mix of modal and sodal is a biblical pattern, as we see in Acts. It is the way the church expresses its nature as the one, holy, catholic and apostolic church; movements and communities like CMS are a key way in which the church can express its apostolic nature. Essentially the teams that led the summer camp and the youth work in chapter one were sodal communities, and the creative and dynamic interplay between the modal and sodal, between these two authentic expressions of church, is vital for mission—after all the members of those teams also belonged to modal communities

Returning to Acts, we discover that 'It was in Antioch that the disciples were first called "Christians"' (11.26). In the astonishing diversity of this rich modality there was nothing else to call them other than 'Christians' because the only thing they had in common was that they were followers of Jesus Christ. It was following Jesus that gave them their fundamental identity. These people, varied as they were, were first and foremost 'Christ people.' In recognizing what made them community in their diversity they realized that the good news of Jesus really was for absolutely *everyone*: for people different from them as well as people like them. And that was why, at this point, they breathe out and set out on mission through the sodality of Paul, Barnabas and John Mark.

One of the most compelling images of the campaign for the abolition of slavery was the image of an enchained slave pleading, 'Am I not a man and a brother?' It was this recognition of our common humanity, which cuts across everything that might otherwise divide us—a recognition of belonging, as it were, to a human modality—that led the founders of CMS both to campaign to abolish slavery and led them outwards, as a sodality, in global mission.

Both sodal and modal modes of Christian community have a key role to play in mission. In this next chapter we will describe how the church particularly as a modality can be better formed for mission. In the last chapter we will examine some specific practices which will help the church, whether modal or sodal, better express its missional calling.

4   The Forgotten Factor

Because we have failed to take into account the sodal and modal aspects of Christian community, and indeed because community has been in itself a neglected factor in our thinking and practice of mission, there is often something quite unbalanced in our commonly held assumptions about how we do church. This chapter is an attempt to rebalance our understanding of community and to demonstrate its inherent missional power.

Back in 1995 Robert Warren, in *Building Missionary Congregations*,[9] talked about three vital dimensions of church life: worship, community, and mission, which he expressed in a Venn diagram[10] as three overlapping circles: circles which equate to the upwards, inwards and outwards dynamics of the life of the church. It was very helpful to find community given equal weight with the other two elements. Robert's main (and very valuable) focus, however, was to encourage us to focus on the crucial intersection between them, where he located a congregation's spirituality.

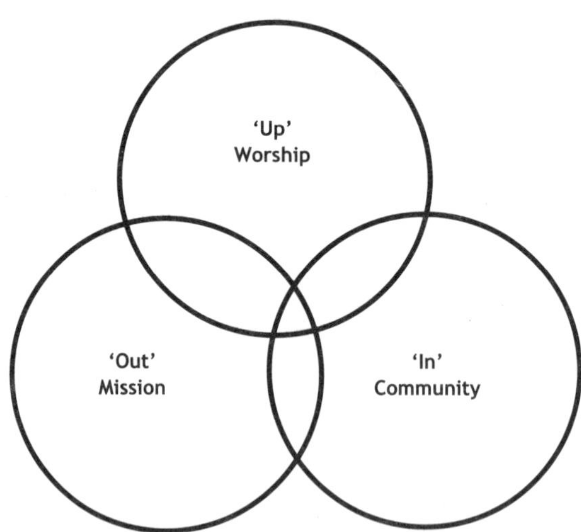

However, this begs the question as to whether this is in fact an accurate reflection of reality in many churches. Perhaps the illustration below equates more closely to the (uncomfortable) reality.

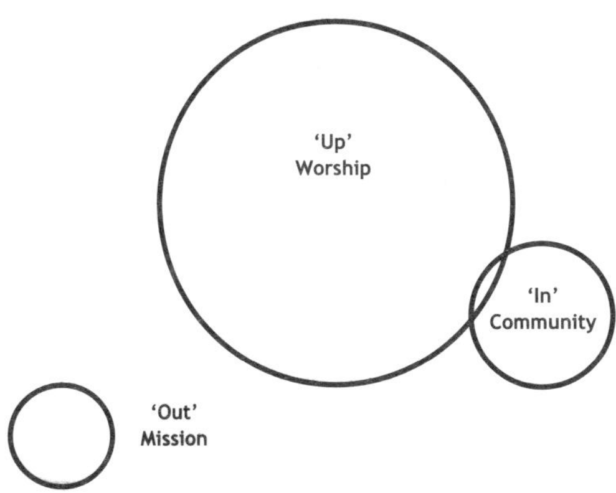

In many churches (though clearly not all) worship, community and mission are seriously out of balance. In an increasingly consumer-orientated culture, churches are often obsessed with what happens on Sunday. And many members are obsessed with whether or not what happens on Sunday meets their expectations. This obsession is not limited to any one tradition: it is true of charismatic churches for whom the quality of the (sung) worship will be critical; it is true of Anglo-catholic churches where Mass must be done 'correctly' and it is true of conservative evangelical churches where so much depends not just on the quality, but also on the style, of the preaching.

For any who doubt this perhaps rather harsh summary, reflect on these two facts. Churches never split over their mission policy, but they frequently have over the nature and style of Sunday worship. Secondly, an analysis of how clergy spend their time will almost certainly reveal that many spend significantly more of their time preparing for the Sunday event than they do investing in the other two circles.

The problem with the model above is not only the neglect of community; it is also the isolation of mission. Mission, in this model, is simply one activity of the life of the church, and not really integral to that life. It is something members of the church community are expected to do, and those members often feel guilty for not engaging in it as they should.

The task we face is to bring these three circles back into balance. Our conviction is that we need to focus far more on our identity as community, and invest in that, taking Acts 2.42–47 as our blueprint (including making sure we spend plenty of time eating together). To do so is not to leave mission in outer orbit. If we invest in community and enlarge that circle then the greater gravitational pull of the community will draw mission back from the margins into the centre.

Although this chapter is mainly concerned with the modal expression of Christian community there is a lesson here for sodal expressions of church too. If sodal expressions are unlikely to fixate on worship (although they might), they can actually fixate on mission themselves, not least by being tied to a particular methodology, or a particular process, or a particular manner of presenting the gospel. The result, ironically, can be the neglect of the people with whom the good news is being shared. One CMS mission partner, when asked what he did to express his mission calling, answered very wisely that whilst he could describe the activities he organizes, 'It's really what happens between them that counts'—by which he meant the investment in people and in community which he makes.

But how does a greater investment in community bring mission back into balance? Let us consider how communities actually work.

There are external dynamics which control any community—things such as rules and regulations—and every community needs them. Churches have them too. Most of these rules are unwritten, but they are nonetheless real: in services we know where we can and cannot go; where we can speak or have to stay silent; when we can sit, stand or kneel. In theological terms these are the constraints of law. And they are important constraints. No community can do without them. But they are not the whole story, not by any means.

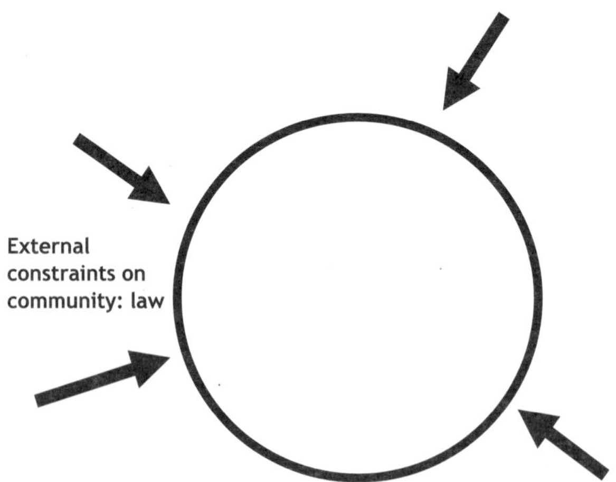

To go back to the summer camp Philip described at the beginning, once the participants had discovered their identity as community, instead of relying on those external dynamics they sought to maximize the dynamics which govern a community from within. And for them, wanting to build a Christian community, those were things such as: love, joy, peace, patience, kindness, goodness, faithfulness, gentleness and self-control—the fruit of the Spirit which Paul lists in Galatians 5. And you can continue the list to include values such as accountability, care, support, justice, compassion. These are distinctively Christian internal dynamics which, even more powerfully than the external ones, hold community together and give it coherence.

To express it theologically, these are the dynamics of grace, and they stand over and against the constraints of law. On their camp the participants set about consciously relying less and less on the external constraints of law and sought to maximize the internal dynamics of grace.

In any human society you cannot do without law—boundaries are always necessary. Historically for Christian communities the creeds have functioned as important boundary markers. But external constraints are never enough, and the best example of a society that is simply controlled by the constraints of law is a prison.

Human communities can be governed by all kinds of internal dynamics, but any community that calls itself Christian has to be governed by these dynamics of grace, because these dynamics are the dynamics of the gospel—hallmarks of the good news of Jesus.

It is undoubtedly a challenge for Christian communities to allow themselves to be shaped by the dynamics of the gospel: to give concrete expression to the gospel, to incarnate the gospel in their community life; to be, in other words, gospel communities. In some way it is easier to rely on law. But churches should not be prisons! And, in the end, relying on the constraints of law is much less fruitful—and much less fruitful in mission not least.

It is less fruitful because something truly significant happens when we focus less on the external constraints of law and more on the internal dynamics of grace. The more we focus on the internal dynamics of grace, the less important the boundary created by the constraints of law becomes. It is in a prison that the boundary is of supreme importance. In communities shaped by grace the boundary matters less. It is not the boundary that defines the community so much as the internal dynamics of grace. It is not how it appears from without that defines it so much as how it is experienced from within.

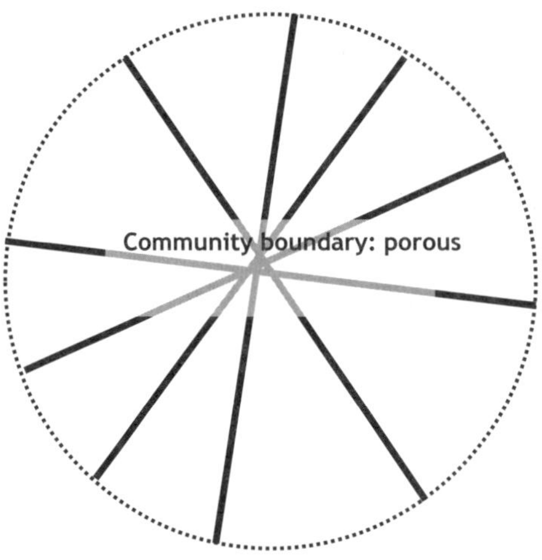

So in communities governed by grace we find that the boundary becomes increasingly porous. And that should not surprise us. The more and the better the community is shaped by grace and the gospel, the more missional that community becomes; not only is it easier to go out from the community with the good news, but it is also easier to enter; both sodal and modal missional expressions become more possible. We find that the boundary between the Christian community and the host community becomes blurred; that should not worry us because it is the internal dynamics of grace, rather than the external boundary, which give the Christian community its identity and integrity. Communities that sit light to law but major on grace are warm, welcoming and attractive places to belong to, easy places to join, and easy places to go out from. They are missional communities we can expect to grow. The challenge we face is to be the builders of just such communities.

5   The Dynamics of Grace

Learn the unforced rhythms of grace.

Matt 11.20–30, *The Message*

A great musician makes playing music look easy, instinctive, soulful and flowing. Yet we all know that this is only a result of hours upon hours of practice, blistered fingers, aching arms etc. Eventually the player is able to relax into the piece, forget the mechanics of playing and begin to feel and speak through the music. But this does not make it any easier; rather, musicians at this level invest themselves more in the music. The music becomes part of them and they of it.

In all of the communities we have experienced—small local communities and large dispersed communities—the struggle to live with and by the dynamics of grace has been one of the steepest learning curves. Community does not just work; it is an ongoing struggle of grace and vulnerability, and it requires intent and determined action. The truth is that in community we discover that living by the dynamics of grace is an act of painful vulnerability, even abandon.

In community we discover that living by grace is an act of painful vulnerability

There is a need to let go and to allow grace to emerge, unforced, as a gift of God and as an expression of our challenge to walk with each other. Walking with God is uncomfortable and messy; it puts us in places we would rather not be with people we struggle with; it shines a light on parts of our lives we would rather keep hidden; it challenges who we think we are and sometimes rips us apart so that we can be reformed. No one is perfect; all of us make a mess of life and all of us see things dimly. At its best community is a place where we can be open and honest about these things, though some bits take longer than others and some are much harder to deal with. As we do this and discover the truth of community we encounter God's character, and indeed God, in new and deeper ways.

Hospitality

Hospitality is a theme that has been referred to with increasing frequency in recent years. There are two sides to hospitality; both are significant and key moments of community life. In the jarring moment when Jesus strips to the waist and sinks to his knees, bowl and towel in hand to wash the feet of his friends and disciples, both sides are present. First, and perhaps most obviously, there is a call to be a good host. The host, in this case Jesus, lowers him or herself voluntarily to the position of servant. Brueggemann explores this in *Living Toward a Vision*, 'The towel and the basin are slavely tools. They do the work no "master" would do *ie* they make contact with the repulsive, abhorrent dimensions of our humanity. The towel and the basin are servant tools. They do the work no reputable competent manager would do—that is they make contact with dimensions of our humanity that need personal caring attention.'[11] Being a good host means opening the door to and kneeling before whomever knocks, no matter how uncomfortable it makes us feel, no matter how hurt or broken they are, no matter how much chaos they bring to our home. There is a fear in letting go, in letting others impact the way we have built our community, but in being a good host it ceases to be 'our' community, the good host hands over ownership and power. Brueggemann goes further when he says, 'The towel and basin are a hard demand for the church from the Lord Jesus. The only trade we can practice is the one for which we have the tools, and the tools he gave on that occasion were the slave tools.'

The second dimension is also there in John 13.1–17: hospitality not only means being a good host; it also means being a good guest. In Luke 10.7–8, the famous mission blueprint, Jesus instructs the seventy-two to 'Stay there, eating and drinking whatever they give you, for the worker deserves his wages. Do not move around from house to house. When you enter a town and are welcomed, eat what is offered to you.' This is no simple instruction, especially for an observer of Jewish law! A good guest does not turn down what is offered, however strange, however alien. A good guest accepts hospitality just as Peter had to accept Jesus' servant act, but Jesus went further when he told them to become a worker, to become part of the family business. In Jeremiah 29 we see a similar instruction from God to the exiled Jewish community, 'Build houses and settle down; plant gardens and eat what they produce. Marry and have sons and daughters; find wives for your sons and give your daughters in marriage, so that they too may have sons and daughters. Increase in number there; do not decrease. Also, seek the peace and prosperity of the city to which I have carried you into exile.' They had to learn how to sing the Lord's song in a strange land and to love and pray for those they found themselves amongst.

Newbigin wrote in *The Gospel in a Pluralist Society*, 'The community of God will be a community that does not live for itself but is deeply involved in the concerns of its neighbourhood. It will be the church for the specific place where it lives, not the church for those who wish to be members of it—or, rather, it will be for them insofar as they are willing to be for the wider community.'[12]

The church Philip led in Paris from 2007–2012 had a significant ministry of hospitality to people who were passing through, often just for a day. The problem he had to address, however, was that church had begun to see this as a problem—and it was indeed costly, having to invest in people for a very short time. The challenge was to help the church embrace this ministry, not as a burden but as a calling. The fruit of this was seen one Thursday when multiple acts of hospitality took place simultaneously in the (rather cramped) building: a memorial service in the sanctuary for a prominent member of the British community; the International Au Pair Café in another room; 'Tea and Listening,' a Bible Study group for older people elsewhere; and in the main hall an asylum advice clinic was being held for refugees from Sri Lanka.

Inclusivity

There comes a point in any community when people move from being a guest to being part of the community. This moment is significant because it means that things have changed. The community is now richer, but just as pruning is painful, so is grafting. The community now has to learn how it has changed and to redefine its space. In community there is no such thing as a junior or a senior member; there are just community members. This does not mean there is no leadership; rather that the role of leadership is different from that in an organization; leadership in community is about including and releasing people. In monastic communities leaders are elected as servants, guardians of the life and vision of the community. Their role is not one of command and control; it is to hold the community to its vision and to ensure that all members are engaged, included and able to participate in its life. In Brueggemann's words: '"The Whole People" bent toward *shalom*, then, is the entire community committed to sharing power with the powerless ones. And that means we must ask who the powerless ones are and how we share the power. The whole people empowering others to share in the wholeness.'[13]

In the summer camp Philip led, many of the leaders had grown up through the camp, and they resisted as far as possible any differentiation between 'junior' and 'senior' leaders: rather, people were grown into responsibility as they were entrusted with leadership. A further result of that was the lines between the leaders and the led were blurred, and the community became increasingly inclusive.

Gifting

'Each of you should use whatever gift you have received to serve others, as faithful stewards of God's grace in its various forms' (1 Pet 4.10). In community each individual must surrender their gifts to the community in order that each person's gift, rather than being lost, becomes anointed for use and spreads through the community. When a prophet is willing to give their insight then all eyes are opened in new ways; when the artist creates, all find new ways to express themselves. In community we move away from organizing mission as a task run by a committee or a team; rather it is an expression and a rhythm of the life of the community. Rather than seeking to build a team with the gifts we need, the mission flows from the community itself—we only have the tools we have been given, and they are enough.

Mark's community in Telford say this about themselves, 'We see the community as itself an embodiment of the kingdom inwardly and outwardly. We seek to reflect *shalom* between ourselves. The community is a small but rich tapestry of Christian expression and churchmanship. We actively allow space for different views and interpretations of the Christian faith in the context of relationship and community. In many ways we believe that part of our charism is to celebrate unity in diversity, to model community rather than club or niche expression. As we live our lives in the wider community we seek to be people of *shalom*, to begin first by offering peace and by living in the wider community as opposed to "reaching out" into it. In a culture where family and community are strained and struggling we believe a major part of a missional response is to model real community and love.'

There are two key stages to gifting. First, to discern the gifting in the community. There are many tools for doing this testing such as the tools provided by Belbin,[14] Myers Briggs[15] and Strength Finder[16]—which can be very helpful in identifying both individual gifts and how a community or team fit together—and more explicitly spiritual tools. A combination of prayer and reflection and practices helping members to identify and articulate their strengths and gifts is a good starting place. However, identifying gifts is only the start. Many churches and communities begin this process but fail to get to the key stage, helping members to practice their gifting in the community and in mission. This can be hugely challenging because it may mean others letting go of roles and activities that they hold to in order to let others play their part. Leadership which allows gifting to flow and flourish needs to be generous leadership, leadership that is willing to give away power and control, and even success.

Generosity and Forgiveness

The Parable of the Prodigal Son is a story about wasteful extravagance (Luke 15.11–32). The focus is normally placed on the son but it is in many ways a story about a wildly and even irresponsibly generous father. The father is generous three times in the story: first in allowing the son both to take his inheritance and to walk away from his responsibilities with the family; secondly, in the giving up of his time and his focus to wait and watch for the son; and thirdly in his fulsome welcome of the son back to the family. The father was lavish in his willingness to let go, his commitment to love despite being abandoned and let down and his unconditional and complete forgiveness leading to total restoration. This is, of course, a picture of divine grace in practice and as such not simply a glimpse of the character of God, but also a challenge to the way we live with others.

One of the great truisms of community life is that it is not easy, and our experiences confirm this. To live in community raises all sorts of challenges; not least of these is that of generosity and forgiveness. A well-known abbot of a monastic community once joked that the first place to look when a kitchen knife was missing was in the backs of the brothers! The reality of community life is that it is not romantic; rather, it is full of struggle and often pain. But in the midst of this we can discover the practice and meaning of grace; we are at times able to grasp the feelings of the father and to learn what it means to live them for others.

One of Philip's iconic moments in ministry came one Maundy Thursday when he offered people the chance either to have their feet washed or to wash the feet of others, depending on their sense of need. Arnold Bolt, an elderly Jamaican man, sat down and took off his shoes and socks and Stephen Bazely, a young white teenager, got up and washed his feet. That in itself was a powerful image. But then without a word spoken between them they simply swapped places and roles. They both understood that their need was both to wash and to be washed; both to give and to receive; both to serve and to be served; both to be host and to be guest.

Their need was both to be host and to be guest

Community of Mission

The Christian community is more than a voluntary association of like-minded people; it is more than a fellowship or friendship group. Theresa of Avila wrote, 'Christ has no body now but yours. No hands, no feet on earth but yours. Yours are the eyes through which he looks compassion on this world. Yours are the feet with which he walks to do good. Yours are the hands through which he blesses all the world. Yours are the hands, yours are the feet, yours are the eyes, you are his body. Christ has no body now on earth but yours.'[17]

For the Christian community this is more than poetic—as Jesus was the means by which God became historically present the church is the continuation of Christ's earthly presence.

As Brueggemann writes, 'The church was fearful of the world because it was so big and hostile and resistant to the gospel. And the image I get from the early church's memory is of a small cringing community quiet in the waiting, waiting and listening, shivering at every siren and nearly fainting at every rap at the door.'[18]

It was to this small, vulnerable community that Jesus promised so much. It was through those men and women huddling together that he promised to reshape the world. It was to them that he issued the invitation to become part of the mission of God. Jesus had prepared them from the very beginning for this mission and the reality of what it meant for them.

> The mission of the church, as the mission of Jesus, involves being sent into the world—to love, to serve, to preach, to teach, to heal, to save, to free.[19]

In *The Forgotten Ways*, Alan Hirsch talks about this common mission in terms of *communitas*, an unstructured state in which all members of a community are equal and with a shared purpose:

> ...inspired to overcome their instincts to 'huddle and cuddle' and to instead form themselves around a common mission that calls them on a dangerous journey to unknown places.[20]

The call of the early Christian community was to open the door, to step out and, as Ann Morisy wrote, 'to rise above the anxiety associated with encountering and embracing a potentially overwhelming, outside world.'[21] This was never an individual task; from the beginning it belonged to a community and it was the dynamic of grace—empowered by the Spirit—which enabled the community to abandon safety, and it was the Spirit that propelled them together out into the world.

Notes

1 John D Zizioulas, *Being as Communion: Studies in Personhood and the Church* (New York: St Vladimir's Seminary Press, 1985).

2 Mike Lowe, *A Church Without Walls* (Grove Pastoral booklet P63).

3 Brian McLaren, *The Church on the Other Side* (Grand Rapids, MI: Zondervan, 2000).

4 David J Bosch, *Transforming Mission* (Maryknoll, NY: Orbis Books, 1991).

5 http://www.undertheiceberg.com/wp-content/uploads/2006/04/Sodality-Winter%20on%20Two%20Structures.pdf

6 Walter Brueggemann, *Living Toward a Vision: Biblical Reflections on Shalom* (Cleveland, OH: United Church Press, 1982).

7 Stephen Bevans, Roger Schroeder (ed), *Constants in Context: A Theology of Mission for Today* (Maryknoll, NY: Orbis, 2004).

8 Samuel Torvend, *Daily Bread, Holy Meal: Opening The Gifts Of Holy Communion* (Minneapolis, MN: Augsburg Fortress Publishing, 2004).

9 Robert Warren, *Building Missionary Congregations* (London: Church House Publishing, 1995).

10 John Venn who designed the Venn diagram, was the son of Henry Venn, General Secretary of CMS, and grandson of CMS' founder, John Venn, Rector of Clapham.

11 Walter Brueggemann, *op cit*.

12 Lesslie Newbigin, *The Gospel in a Pluralist Society* (Grand Rapids, MI: Eerdmans, 1989).

13 Walter Brueggemann, *op cit*.

14 http://www.belbin.com

15 http://www.myersbriggs.org

16 https://www.gallupstrengthscenter.com

17 http://spckpublishing.co.uk/blog/spck-prayer/prayers-of-st-teresa-of-avila-1515-1582/

18 Walter Brueggemann, *op cit*.

19 Joseph Petulla, *Christian Political Theology* (Maryknoll, NY: Orbis Books, 1972).

20 Alan Hirsch, *The Forgotten Ways* (Grand Rapids, MI: Brazos Press, 2006).

21 Ann Morisy, *Journeying Out* (London: Continuum, 2004).